Story Time with Edgar Cayce

Written by Karla Peterson
with Leslie Cayce

Illustrated by Karla Peterson

Story Time with Edgar Cayce

Copyright © 2020 Karla Peterson and Leslie Cayce

All rights reserved. No part of this book may be reproduced in any form or by any electronic or mechanical means, including information storage and retrieval systems, without permission in writing from the publisher, except by reviewers, who may quote brief passages in a review.

ISBN 978-0-578-66968-7 (Paperback edition)

Back cover: photograph, Edgar Cayce and Thomas Jefferson Davis, ECF1031, 1939; E.C.F. Photographic Collection, Acc. 3, The Edgar Cayce Foundation, Virginia Beach, VA. Used with permission.

Printed and bound in the United States of America

First Printing: April 2020

Published by Karla Peterson and Leslie Cayce

Available at Amazon.com

For more information about the life and on-going work of Edgar Cayce
visit www.edgarcayce.org or
The Association for Research and Enlightenment
215 67th Street, Virginia Beach, VA 23451
800-333-4499

*This book is dedicated to
our real grandchildren,
Lily, River, Eleanor, Juniper,
Ryan, James, Aurelia, and Bodhi,
and to all children,
with love*

CHAPTER 1

With a contented sigh, Edgar Cayce cast his fishing line into the lake behind his house. He loved fishing. He had spent the morning working in his garden. But now it was hot, so he sat waiting for a fish to bite, enjoying the cool shade on his pier.

Hearing the cheerful sounds of children on the path nearby, his kind face broke into a grin. "Well, hello there friends, how good to see you again!" he called out. "Have you come to keep me and the fish company?"

Lily, the oldest, spoke up shyly, "Actually, Mr. Cayce, we were hoping you might tell us some more stories about your life."

Edgar smiled even more, for he loved children and especially this group of eight. He enjoyed their energy and their questions. And he always loved sharing about his unusual life.

"So, you want to hear more of my stories, do you?" he asked. "Well then, I'll just give the fish a bit of a rest. Why don't we all sit over there on the grass?"

He set aside his fishing rod and sat beneath a tall shade tree. The children settled happily around him.

"Will you tell us about when you were little, please, Mr. Cayce?" River asked.

Edgar's eyes twinkled, "Sure I will, if you'll promise to call me Judge, instead of Mr. Cayce. That's what my good friends call me, and you are my good friends." The children liked that very much.

"Let's see, where shall I start?" He looked at their trusting faces. "How about if I tell you about my grandfather? It was a long time ago and a little sad, but it all turned out just fine."

And so Edgar Cayce began. "Until I was four, my favorite thing of all was to spend time with my grandfather. Even before I could talk, I

loved him best. They say I used to sleep over at my grandparents' house when I was pretty little. Tucked in the bed with them, if I woke in the night, my little fingers would search in the dark for cheeks with a beard. Once I found Grandpa's chin whiskers," he chuckled, "why then, I'd snuggle up to him and fall right back to sleep.

"My grandparents had a beautiful tobacco farm in Kentucky and my family lived nearby. There were rolling green fields and a big vegetable garden. I loved exploring it. Best of all was when Grandpa and I went riding on his horse. I loved sitting up on that big horse in front of my grandfather, with his strong arms wrapped around me. We'd check the tobacco plants. And when it got too hot, we'd stop by the river to fish. He's the one who taught me to fish you know, when I was pretty little. I loved his stories about when he was a boy. We laughed a bunch. He was my best friend.

"Then suddenly, something real sad happened. We'd been out riding and were hot, so we went to the pond to give his horse a drink. Grandpa put me down so I could hunt for frogs while he watered the horse. But then, out of the blue, his horse got spooked and reared up on its hind legs. My grandfather was knocked right out of the saddle and into the pond. He must have hit his head, because he didn't get back up again. 'Grandpa!' I shouted, but he didn't move. Like a flash, I went running and calling for help.

Men rushed over, but by the time they got to him, my grandfather had died."

The children grew still, watching him closely.

"Were you very sad?" Juniper asked, quiet and serious.

"And were you a little scared?" added River.

"I *was* scared and so sad, as sad as you can imagine being, for I'd lost the person I loved the most. And I was really lonely after that. Even though I was close to my sisters and especially my mother, no one could replace my grandfather.

"But after a few months, the strangest thing happened. I was outside playing when I thought I saw my grandfather walking into the barn. So I peeked inside, and yep, there he was!"

"Wait a minute, I'm confused," Ryan objected. "I thought you said he died?"

"Well, yes," Edgar explained slowly, "indeed he did. But here's the funny thing: I could kind of see right through him, like he wasn't solid anymore. Yet it really was him! He turned, smiled just like he always did, and walked right over to me. 'Don't worry, Old Man,' he said (that was his special name for me). 'Even though my body died, my spirit is still alive and well. I'm watching over you. Whenever you need me, I'll be nearby.'

"I sure liked that! I started to think of him as my very own guardian angel. After that, he and I talked in that barn pretty often, so I didn't feel quite so lonely.

"You see, I'd always liked stories about angels, and he felt like my own angel. I especially loved stories about Jesus and God. I listened very carefully to the Bible stories the preacher told in church. Once I could read, I even wished for a Bible of my very own. In those days, children didn't have many books of their own to read.

"Do y'all have books at home?" he asked them.

"I do!" exclaimed little Bodhi.

"Reading is one of my favorite things," Lily admitted.

"I love to get books at the library," added James.

"Well, see how lucky you are?" Edgar was enjoying himself.

"One day," he continued, "my father told Mr. Hopper, the owner of our little town bookstore, that I was wishin' for a Bible. So Mr. Hopper decided to give me one as a present, one that fit right in my pocket! He said that any child who wanted their own Bible should have one. You just don't know how happy that made me. I started to read my Bible right away, even though some of the words were hard for me. But my wonderful mother helped me figure them out, and pretty soon I carried that book around all the time.

"My favorite stories were about Jesus. He was amazing, a great teacher, filled with the spirit of God. He understood God and was the kindest of men. And He could do incredible things, miracles really, like walk on water and heal sick people. Do you know anyone who can do things like that?" Edgar asked.

The group solemnly shook their heads.

"Well," said Edgar. "Jesus could do that and more. He taught about the power and love of God. And even though He did all those miraculous things, He explained that it was really the God force in him that did it. And He said that same force is in all of us – each of you, right here!

"Jesus especially loved children, just like you. He would sit with them, like we are now, telling stories about how to treat each other with loving kindness. He taught that everyone is a child of God, even grown-ups. And that people everywhere are really brothers and sisters, like one big family, in their hearts.

"Our main job, He said, is to be kind, helpful, and loving. And to forgive anyone who makes us mad or hurts us. He especially wanted children to know that when they were scared or needed Him, all they had to do was close their eyes and think about love. That way His spirit was there for them.

"And even though His body died long ago, Jesus can still be the best of friends and a teacher for every one of you. I know," Edgar said quietly, "because that's just what He is to me."

CHAPTER 2

A breeze rustled the leaves as Edgar began another story. Some of the children were making fairy houses with sticks and leaves.

"When I was a boy," he said, "I loved all the amazing stories in my Bible. They were not just stories to me, they were very real. I liked to read Bible stories aloud to my parents before bed. My favorite place to read was a quiet spot by the creek, a little retreat I'd built. I'd go there after chores to read my Bible. One day, I had been reading and praying real hard that God would show me that He loved me, and that I could do something that would show others His love.

"That night I had my first vision. I was almost asleep when I felt as if I was being lifted up. A glorious light, like the rising morning sun, seemed to fill my room as a figure appeared at the foot of my bed. I thought it must be my mother and called to her. I even got up and went to her, but no, it wasn't Mother. For a moment I was frightened. I returned to my bed, and almost immediately the figure appeared again. Then, it seemed all gloriously bright."

He paused to ask the children, "So who do you think it was?"

Eleanor spoke right up, "An angel!" She looked a bit like one herself.

"Yes, Eleanor," Edgar replied, "I think he *was* an angel! And this is what he said, 'Thy prayers are heard. You will have your wish. Remain faithful. Be true to yourself. Help the sick, the afflicted.'

"I was so surprised, and excited, all rolled into one! But I knew that most people would not believe that I'd really seen an angel. Mother often said she didn't know why people had trouble believing that the amazing things in the Bible couldn't happen today. When I told her about the angel, she believed me! She hugged me and said I had received a very special gift. But we kept my angel visit a secret between us.

"You see, living out in the country like we did, I didn't have many friends, except for my best friend, Anna, and my 'invisible playmates.'

Mother called them that because most folks couldn't see them, just like no one else could see my grandfather after he died. But my mother, Anna and I could see them alright, and talk with them, too."

Now the children listened more closely.

"When our invisible playmates came to play, we chased each other in the orchard and slid down piles of hay. It was such fun! But if anyone else came around, poof! They vanished.

"Sometimes it bothered me that we were the only ones who saw them. When I told my grandmother about them, she said not to worry, that I had the gift of second sight. That meant I knew and saw things most others couldn't. She said my grandfather had it, too, and that made me feel a whole lot better. She told me that there was nothing wrong with having unusual powers, as long as I used them for God's work. So, I just enjoyed playing with Anna and 'the little people', as we called them."

While Edgar spoke, Lily had pulled a small sketchbook from her pocket and started to draw. She especially liked to draw angels. Eleanor watched her closely.

Edgar did too, then continued, "I was sad when Anna moved away. I didn't have any regular school friends. My little country school had just one room for students of all ages. And I wasn't such a good student. I think my mind used to wander during class. It was really hard for me to concentrate and learn my lessons.

"Well, the very next night after I saw the angel, another unusual thing happened. I was trying to study my spelling words, but they just would not stick in my mind. Have any of you ever had that problem?" he asked.

"I have," said Ryan, nodding.

"Me, too," murmured Eleanor.

"Lots of folks do," said Edgar. "My father was trying to help me, but I was getting tired. That's when I heard the voice of my angel again, saying, 'Sleep and we may help you.'

"So I asked Father, 'May I just sleep for a few minutes and then we can try these words again?' He was very frustrated with me, but he let me lay my head down on those books.

"Sure enough, I fell fast asleep. Soon Father came back and shook me awake. He asked me to spell the first word and that's when the most surprising thing happened. I saw that word perfectly in my mind and spelled it right out! He had me spell the next word and the next. Seems I could now spell all the words on the list! He thought I'd been making fun of him and knocked me out of my chair. But I got back up and said, 'Really, Father, ask me any of the words in my spelling book, I think I can spell them all now!' And you know what? I could!

"Have you ever tried doing something like that?" Edgar asked.

"Never," Aurelia said, shaking her head slowly.

"It surely was amazing," he mused. "From that day on, I would read my lesson, sleep on it awhile, then spell every word, as if I was reading with my eyes open! You can bet I did much better in school after that. But of course, I still had to figure out all the math problems for myself," he chuckled.

"My teachers and the other children did not know what to make of me. They thought I was a very strange boy indeed. And perhaps I was. I know I sure got teased a lot. But Mother and Grandma said I'd been given a gift, and I believed them. Even though I was sad sometimes not to have more friends, I felt in my heart that God had something special for me to do in life."

"What did God want you to do?" Juniper repeated softly.

"Well," replied Edgar, "it helps if you understand something about God. But my friends, isn't that enough for today?"

He was right. The children bounded up, thanking him. Edgar stretched his long legs. Picking up his hat and fishing rod, he took his time, examining his garden on the way.

CHAPTER 3

Before long the children returned to Edgar's tree. Their older gentleman friend set aside his garden shovel and joined them there.

"I believe we were fixin' to talk a bit about God," Edgar began. "We often speak as if God were a person, but really, God is not a person. It is more like a spirit or a force inside us. I venture to say that it is the Life Force, powerful, yet gentle and comforting. So much more than a person!

"Native Americans say it's the Great Spirit in every single thing on earth. God is nature, and nature is God, the energy that drives the ocean waves, the wind and the clouds across the sky, bringing the rain. It's the energy deep in the earth that bursts forth as flowers and leaves on trees. We can see the beauty and feel the wonder of God all around us in nature!

"God is also love. And love is God. I know, it's confusing! Imagine, this same Life Force, this great love, is within you, too! It created your spirits long ago, before you were born. And someday, after your body dies, the exciting thing is that your spirit will live on! It will go home to the heavenly garden, to that loving Oneness we call God.

"Just remember, this loving, Creative Force not only created you, but knows you, treasures you, and loves you, just as you are. And can guide you, if you choose to listen." Edgar paused, appreciating the open faces of the children, even as they started to squirm. It was time for a change, so he switched to another story.

"Have I told you about when I got hit with a baseball?" he asked, tickling those nearest him with blades of grass. He had told them this one and it was one of their favorites. River wiggled closer. He loved all games with a ball.

"I wasn't very good at sports," Edgar said. "At recess, I'd rather talk with my teachers about the mysteries of life than play with the others. But one day, I was playing a ball game called Old Sower. It's like baseball and tag. That day, the ball hit me on my back, right here." He showed them the spot. "After that, they say I acted real strange, giggling and making faces. My sister even had to lead me home.

"When I got home, seems I threw things at the table and made faces at my father. Believe me, that was not normal for me, so Mother finally put me to bed. I don't remember any of this. They say I pulled up the covers and slowly relaxed. Then I told my parents that my body was suffering from shock after being hit by that ball. And to put a poultice of cornmeal, onions and herbs on the back of my head. I said that I would be alright by morning if they did that.

"Well, they were surprised, of course, but they knew a poultice would not hurt me, so they did as I said. At last, I fell asleep. Next morning, I felt fine! Everyone was so relieved I was back to my normal, healthy self. Even Father was proud of me because I had cured myself. He told people I was the greatest fellow in the world…when I was asleep! I wasn't sure how I'd cured myself, but I was mighty happy to feel normal again."

"That's amazing!" said River, shaking his head. "But … what is a poultice?"

That amused Edgar because, even after all this time, he had to agree, it was amazing! And of course, the children didn't know what a poultice was, they weren't used much anymore. He explained that a poultice is cloth wrapped around different herbs, plants or foods that can heal. Then he went on.

"My family did not have much money, you see, so after eighth grade, I quit school to help my uncle on the farm. I lived with my dear grandmother while the rest of my family moved to town so my father could work, and my sisters could go to school. I was only sixteen, and I sure missed them!

"Once, after working in the fields all day, I rode back to the barn on the mule that pulled my plow. Well, I didn't know it, but no one else could ride that ol' mule without getting kicked off. I had no problem with her though, and when one of the workers saw that, he wanted to ride the mule, too. Don't you know, that cranky mule kicked him right off, which was pretty funny, I had to admit."

Edgar chuckled as the children burst out laughing at James pretending to kick like a mule.

He continued, "Everyone wondered how I was able to ride her. The men all looked at me like I was a pretty strange fellow, which made me uncomfortable. I didn't like feeling odd. I just wanted to be an ordinary boy!

"I stayed there for a year to be with my grandmother, and I was with her when she died. Soon after, I was fixin' a plow when I heard a voice. I turned, and there was my angel! 'Leave your plow,' he said. 'Go be near your mother. She needs you. A way will be provided. Go now.' Well, I quit my job that very day and walked thirteen miles to be with my family again."

"Wow!" River erupted in surprise. He liked running fast and far. It wasn't easy, so he couldn't imagine walking thirteen miles.

Edgar nodded. "I needed a new job, so I went to see Mr. Hopper at the bookstore. He remembered me as that little boy who'd wanted his own Bible. I told him that I was fixin' to read my Bible from the beginning to the end, every year, which is a big job because it's long, and hard to understand. And I told him that I'd already read it many times. Well, he liked the sound of that. And then I borrowed the store's book catalog from him. It listed all the books in the store. Sure enough, after I slept on that catalog, I knew the name and author of every single book! Mr. Hopper liked that, too, so he gave me a job.

"It was quite a change, from working as a farm hand to being a clerk in town. But you know what? I really liked working in the bookstore and helping people. I worked hard and learned to work with customers. I never went back to school, even though I wanted to. But the money I earned helped my family and that made me happy.

"Soon I grew more comfortable around people, and less shy. I even made some friends. By then I knew the Bible so well that I was asked to teach Sunday School at church. I loved that. You see, Bible stories were my favorite subject, and children seemed to enjoy hearing my stories about God and Jesus."

"Just like us!" Ryan piped up. "We love your stories."

"We sure do," agreed James.

"Then, my friends," Edgar said, "come back soon for more, okay?"

His garden was calling him and he could tell the children were itching to play some baseball.

Their happy voices trailed behind them, "Bye, Judge! Thank you!"

CHAPTER 4

When the group returned, Edgar had a question for them, "Do any of you remember your dreams?"

"I do! I do!" Aurelia and Ryan excitedly waved their arms, forgetting they weren't in school. The older ones understood and smiled.

"Me, too," Edgar was smiling, too. "One night when I was a teenager, I had a very special dream where I walked to a river and stood near a young woman. A veil covered her face, and she held my hand. Our joined hands were covered by a long gold cloth. I knew she was very special, though I didn't recognize her. In the morning, I asked my mother what the dream might mean. She suggested I search the Bible. We wondered if this woman wore a veil because I had not met her yet. And since our hands were joined, maybe we were supposed to be together. I treasured that dream. I thought that someday this young woman might become my wife.

"But guess what?" he paused. "Turns out that I dreamed about that veiled woman 57 more times during my life! It's true! That was just the first time. Now I wonder if she is more like a guardian angel for me, like my grandfather.

"I know dreams are hard to understand sometimes, but they're important helpers for us. Did you know that everyone dreams, every night," Edgar went on, "even though sometimes we don't remember them? Dreams are like stories told by your wise, inner self. Sometimes they help with your problems. Sometimes they show you things you need to learn. In many dreams, everything is like a part of yourself to listen to or learn more about.

"And you know what else? Even though some dreams may seem frightening, they are all only trying to help you, to point you in the right direction. Dreams are your friends, like having your own inner teacher at night. Plus, it's fun trying to remember them!"

The children were lying on their backs, with dreamy looks on their faces.

"Well," he went on, "after that dream with the veiled woman, I did meet a lovely young woman named Gertrude. She was 15 and I was 17

years old. She was gentle, kind, and pretty, too. Her big family lived in a beautiful home on a hill outside town. Lucky for me, they all liked me, and didn't think me strange at all. Neither did Gertrude. We could talk about everything. It was so easy between us. Before long, any time you'd see Gertrude, I'd be close by. I grew to love her very much. But it took years until I got up the courage to ask her to marry me. And you know what? She made me wait a whole week before she finally said, 'Yes!'"

The group sighed. "They loved each other," Juniper told the others.

"And we still do!" Edgar laughed. "But one big thing stopped us from getting married. Money. I did not make enough money to take care of us. So I decided to move to the big city. I hoped to earn more working in a bigger bookstore. The only problem was that the city bookstore didn't need workers right then. But I didn't give up. I asked folks back home to write letters saying nice things about me. I sent two of those letters to that bookstore owner every day. And you know what? He finally hired me!"

"Oh good," Lily smiled.

"Yes," River agreed, "I was getting nervous for you."

Edgar affectionately ruffled his golden curls as he continued. "Just like before, I slept on his catalog of books, and learned the name and author of every book they had. Soon he was very happy he'd hired me. Even though I really missed my family and Gertrude, I liked working in that bookstore and met lots of interesting people.

"After awhile, I felt it was time to move back home to be near the people I loved. My father had a new job by then, so I started working with him. I had to travel a lot and be outdoors in bad weather. I think it made me sick.

"Then another really strange thing happened. I lost my voice! I mean, it just wouldn't come back. And guess what? It's hard to sell anything if you only whisper. I tried everything to get my voice back, but nothing worked. None of the doctors could help me either."

He looked at the group, "Have you ever tried to go a whole day only whispering?"

"That would be really hard," said James. The others nodded. They all loved to talk, even little Bodhi.

"Yes, indeed!" Edgar exclaimed. "Really hard! And I couldn't speak for a whole year! Once again, I had to find another job, one where I didn't need to talk. Finally, a photographer hired me. He talked with the customers, I took pictures and it worked out really well. I liked taking pictures very much and got quite good at it.

"Then something happened that totally changed my life. But I think I'll tell you about it next time," Edgar teased.

"No, no!" the children protested. "Tell us now, Judge, please?"

"Oh well, okay," said Edgar, pleased with himself. He did like to tease. "Here's what happened. One day, a hypnotist came to town, and he heard that I'd lost my voice. He said if he could hypnotize me, I would talk again. I wasn't even sure what 'hypnotize' meant. Do you know? I found out - it means that when our minds are between asleep and awake, they are more open. That's when a hypnotist can make suggestions and our minds are very open to them.

"Well, I was pretty desperate by then, and ready to try anything, so I let him try. And he said to me, 'Relax now and go to sleep.' But you know what? It didn't work. So I put myself to sleep, just like when I slept on my schoolbooks. And then, it seemed to work. Even though I looked like I was asleep, I answered his questions in my normal voice! But there was one big problem. When I woke up, I could still only whisper. Now that was very frustrating!

"What do you think was going on?" he asked, looking at each child.

"I don't know," Lily was puzzled. "How could you answer questions when you were asleep? We can't do that. And if you could speak when you were asleep, why couldn't you speak when you were awake?"

"Yes, I know," replied Edgar, remembering how baffled they were at the time. "We surely didn't understand either. Soon I put myself in that in-between state again. This time, when the hypnotist asked me what was going on, I told him to tell my body to send more blood to my throat. He did and they tell me that the skin all around my throat got really red. After a few minutes, I told him that was enough. And this time when I woke up again, I could talk!

"Well, we were all so excited, you can't imagine! It had been so long since I could speak above a whisper! We soon learned that somehow, even though I looked like I was sleeping, I wasn't. But I wasn't awake either! We realized that somehow my body knew what it needed to heal itself. If someone asked me to explain what was going on, I could answer, in my normal voice, even though it looked like I was sleeping. Very strange, right? After awhile, I figured it must be part of the special powers my mother and grandmother had told me about long ago.

"And when I woke up that day, I didn't remember what happened in that almost-sleep state. I still can't. And that made us very nervous, especially me. Plus, I certainly did not know the answers to those questions when I was awake. I am not a doctor!"

"That is so strange, kind of like magic," Eleanor said, almost to herself. They were each picturing Judge's throat turning red.

"Indeed," Edgar agreed. "And that, my friends, is a good stopping place for today. It's a lot even for grown-ups to understand."

The children walked home more slowly this time.

CHAPTER 5

Soon they returned, hoping Judge would say more about his sort-of-sleep. And he did.

"Yes, I sure was happy to have my voice back. But I was also very confused. What had happened to me? Was this something I could do again? Was it something I wanted to do again? And you know what? I was kind of afraid to find out. No one I knew could do that sort of thing. Was it a gift from God? Or was it something scary that I shouldn't do?"

Edgar looked closely at them. "What do you think you would do?" he asked.

Lily had given it some thought and replied, "I think if someone was hurt and needed help, I'd try to see if I could do it again."

Edgar was moved. "Lily, that beautiful answer shows how you care about others. I wanted to help others, too, but I was scared, feeling different all over again, when all I really wanted was to be normal. So at first, I didn't do anything. I just kept those confusing questions to myself and kept taking photographs. But soon it seemed that God had other plans for me.

"You see, people heard about how I'd cured myself and started asking if I could try the same thing for them. One was Gertrude's cousin Carrie. Her baby, Tommy, was real sick. His doctors said he would die soon. Carrie was so upset and scared. She asked if I would go to sleep to see why the baby was so sick, just like I did when I couldn't talk. I was afraid I'd say something when I was almost asleep that would hurt the baby. But Carrie was very strong and sure. She trusted and believed in me. If the baby was going to die anyway, she said, how could it hurt?

"So finally, I agreed and stretched out on a bed. Someone wrote down and read out the words about helping this baby's body and I fell right into that almost-sleep state. When asked about the baby, again I seemed to know what would help. I said to give him a certain medicine and to make him a peach-tree poultice."

"Wow!" exclaimed Aurelia. "How did you know to do that, Mr. Judge?" The others, and Edgar, smiled at that.

"That's just how I felt, Aurelia, how *did* I do that?" Edgar mused. "When I woke up, they had to tell me what I'd said for baby Tommy because I didn't remember a thing. And it was scary, because the medicine I had described? We all knew it was poisonous if you took too much. I did not want to give him the medicine if there was any chance it could hurt him. But Carrie was certain they should do exactly what my sleeping-self said. So they did.

"Well, don't you know, that very night, the baby started getting better! Carrie and her family were so excited! It seemed like a miracle. But, children," he paused, "how do you think I felt?"

Once again, Lily spoke thoughtfully, "I think you were very happy the baby was okay. But maybe you were all mixed up about your special powers."

"Yes, that's just it, Lily!" Edgar was impressed. "I didn't know what to do with this power, or gift, whatever you call it. I didn't know anyone else who could do it. And that really scared me. I did not want to hurt anyone, I wanted only to help.

"Eventually, I remembered the angel had said that I should help people who were sick. I decided that maybe this is what he meant. At that time, I did not go looking for people to help, but after that, folks started finding me. It was then that I made this promise to myself and my family: if I ever said anything when I was 'sleeping' that hurt anyone, I'd never do another of these readings. That's what we call them, 'readings.'"

"What is a reading, actually?" asked Ryan.

"And how do you do it?" James asked.

"Friends," said Edgar, "let's start there next time. Help me remember, okay?" It was lunchtime. Everyone stood up. Then suddenly, startling Edgar, they took turns shaking his hand or bowing or curtsying in solemn farewell. James saluted, and then they all took off.

"Blessings, y'all!" he called, slowly waving his hat.

"You, too, Judge … you, too," their voices trailed after them.

CHAPTER 6

Before long, they gathered again beneath the shade tree. Little Bodhi crept shyly into Edgar's lap and reached up to pat his face. Edgar loved that.

"As I recall," said Edgar, "you asked me what a reading is, Ryan, so let me explain. Here's what I do. First, I lie down and get real quiet. Like I said, it's sort of like sleep, but different. Sometimes, it's like my mind up and leaves my body and goes to a huge library, where an old man hands me a large book, which is like a record of the person asking the questions. I call this a Book of Life."

The children's eyes widened, imagining an old man with a thick book.

"I read from it," Edgar continued, "and the answers are there, for the spirit of God and our own inner selves know everything about us.

Once I find the answers, why then my voice speaks. But when my body wakes up, I do not recall a single thing.

"I still really don't know *how* it works and it's not always the same, sometimes there's no Book of Life. But you know how a radio seems to pick up its sounds from the air? How does it do that? I wonder if I'm somehow like a radio and get tuned to a higher source that knows what someone needs. Kind of curious, don't you think?" he asked.

"Yes. But kind of magical, too," Eleanor said dreamily. Aurelia's head rested on Juniper's shoulder for a moment.

"I wish I could do that!" Ryan said. "Can you tell us how?"

Edgar laughed, "Well, you know, I still don't understand it fully, but I think it may have something to do with listening to God."

"How do we do that?" asked James.

"Remember how God is inside of you?" Edgar asked. "One way to get to know this God energy better is just to be quiet and listen for a still, small voice inside you that's your own connection to that Spirit. Another way is spending quiet time alone outside in nature. Or praying that others get the help they need. Or practicing being kind and patient.

"Let's try something, children. Everyone lie on your backs and get real comfortable. Close your eyes … but hey, no falling asleep!" he joked.

"Now breathe in and out slowly. Imagine a light glowing around and inside of you. Breathe it in and out of your heart. Let it fill your whole body. As you breathe, say to yourself, 'Kindness is love, kindness is love.'"

His eyes rested on each one, seeing them relax and become peaceful. After a few minutes, he spoke softly, "Now take another deep breath and send that light to someone who is sad or someone you love. See them filled with your white light."

After a moment, he said quietly, "Now open your eyes. How do you feel?"

James spoke slowly, "I feel as light as a bird."

"I feel like a tall tree, with energy coming up from my roots and out through my leaves," said Lily.

"I feel as strong and bright as the sun," Aurelia added.

"Me, too," Juniper chimed in.

"I'm a butterfly!" exclaimed Bodhi, spreading out his arms like wings.

Edgar was excited. "Oh, I like all this! This is called meditation. Getting quiet, letting the light of the Great Spirit flow through your body. It is always there for you, all you have to do is be quiet and listen."

The children lay back a moment longer watching clouds race by. Soon Ryan sat up and asked, "Please, Judge, what else did you say when you were almost-asleep?" The others sat up too, reaching for their water bottles.

"Well," Edgar said, smiling, "like I said, over the years, folks usually asked for my help when their doctors could no longer help them. They wanted to see if I had some answers. I would lie down on my couch in a quiet room, loosen my tie, take off my shoes, and relax into that almost-asleep state.

"My wife, Gertrude, was the best one to sit beside me. She gave me special instructions, then asked questions for the person who needed help. Our wonderful secretary, Miss Gladys, wrote down all my answers. Good thing, too, because when we were finished, and I woke up, I didn't recall anything I'd said. I would ask, 'Did we get a good one?' I was awfully glad to read her notes. And over the years we did *thousands* of these readings!"

"Whoa!" Lily was impressed. She asked, "How did it make you feel, being able to help people like that?"

Edgar paused. Here was another good question from this bunch.

"I felt like I just had to try to help others when they asked. But to be honest, sometimes I still felt rather ashamed of the whole performance."

"But you helped so many people," River protested. "Hey, did you tell anyone how to stay strong and healthy?"

"Actually, yes," said Edgar. "For example, one of the best ways is by eating plenty of fresh vegetables and fruits, especially right from the garden. What do you like to eat from your vegetable gardens?"

"My favorites are strawberries, and peas I can pop open!" exclaimed James.

"I love red peppers and radishes," said Aurelia.

"And carrots and kale," Ryan added.

Eleanor quietly confessed, "Actually, I could eat tomatoes forever." Her little sister, Juniper, nodded. It was true.

Edgar laughed. "Those delicious things are fun to eat right in the garden! People were encouraged to eat foods just like those. Also, whole grains, nuts and seeds, beans, fish, chicken. And to drink eight to ten cups of water every day!"

"Wow, that's a lot of water," said River, reaching again for his water bottle.

"But what about cookies and ice cream?" Juniper's mind was clearly elsewhere.

Edgar loved how children thought. "Well, most people would do well not to eat very many of those foods. Why do you think that is?" he asked.

"Too much sugar," said Lily, shaking her head. She knew how she felt when she ate too much of it, and it wasn't good.

"Indeed," he said. "Too much — even of a good thing - is still too much!

"Sometimes my 'almost-asleep self' suggested special exercises and massages. I know you like to run around a lot. Do any of you like having your feet massaged?" he asked.

"I love it," said Aurelia.

"Me, too!" added Bodhi.

Edgar smiled, "So do I. These readings tried to bring each person's body back into balance, using natural healing treatments to heal itself. And you know what? Most of the time, *if* people did what was suggested, they got a lot better! Over and over again! It always amazed me. They were very thankful. And I was grateful to help in this way, because it felt like God's work."

CHAPTER 7

"What else was in those notes Miss Gladys took?" asked River.

"Let's see," Edgar said. "Some folks asked what sort of work would be best for them. Others were surprised to hear they needed to forgive someone. Or to work on their attitude. Do you know what 'attitude' means?"

Ryan spoke right up. "I think it means you get to choose. You can be mad or you can be glad. I can choose to hit my brother when he makes me mad. Or I can walk away and do something fun by myself instead. My mother always tells me I get to choose whether I have a good attitude or a bad one."

"And which kind of attitude makes you feel better?" Edgar wondered.

Ryan looked up grinning. "A good one, of course, because it just feels … good!"

Edgar nodded. "That's what the readings say too, Ryan. Be thankful for what you have, and you will be happy. It's that simple."

"Even when my sister takes my toys?" Eleanor was serious.

"Well now," Edgar looked at them, "there's a tough one. Can any of you think of something for Eleanor to be happy about when Juniper takes her toys?"

The children all knew what that felt like. James asked, "She could be happy she has nice toys?"

Aurelia, who had a sweet little brother but no sister, added, "She could be glad she has a sister?"

Edgar smiled. "Good ones! That's just the idea. Attitude is everything. And you know what? We might even pick our sisters and brothers and our parents before we're born!

"Ryan, you might have known James was going to be your brother before either of you were born. What do you think of that?"

Now Ryan was confused. "Did I also know that he'd play with my toys so much?"

Edgar said, "Maybe. Like I said, we all have a body, but we also have a spirit. And our spirits may have been here before and remember things. Our spirits may also come back again in a new body, in the future. So we may get to live more than once."

He gave that a moment to sink in. This was tricky to explain.

"Sometimes, the readings told people that they had lived before, in a different body and a different place. And told them what they had to learn from those other lives. And that people might choose to be born to be together again. Like with families. Why? So we can love, forgive, teach, and learn more from each other again.

"In this lifetime, you might be a son or daughter, but in another life, your mama or papa might have been your child! If you spanked your child a lot in your last life, they may come back as your parent this time, to show you how bad it feels to be spanked. Or if your brother is mean to you in this life, maybe you were mean to him in another lifetime. Does that make a little sense?" he asked.

The children were fidgeting. After all, Edgar thought, this was hard for adults, too. He tried saying it another way.

"Sometimes you have a girl's body, and sometimes a boy's body. But our spirits are not a boy or a girl. Our bodies are, but our spirits are not. We can learn a lot by being a girl in one life, and by being a boy in another. I bet that we have also had black, brown, or white skin in other lifetimes. And have lived in different countries, and spoken different languages. It's fun to imagine, don't you think?" he asked.

They still looked uncertain, so he decided, "That's a-plenty for today, I think." The group jumped up, ready to play.

"Bye for now, friends," Edgar called, stretching his legs. He watched Bodhi and Juniper, their curls bouncing, as they caught up with the others.

CHAPTER 8

Late one afternoon, Aurelia and the children practiced skipping along the path to see Edgar.

As they settled in, he asked, "Have y'all been thinking about those past lives we talked about? When the readings first described them, we sure talked about it a lot, trying hard to understand. Past lives had never occurred to us before."

"*Why* do we have more than one life?" River asked.

"That's a good question, River," said Edgar. "I've actually studied that some. Some say it's our choice to come back because there's too much to learn and do in one lifetime! We're born with talents that may be from our past lives. Each person is unique, with different experiences and different lessons to learn. We have so many chances to learn in each lifetime. We all do! And every single thing that happens to us can teach us, if we chose to let it. We all have so much to learn, especially kindness, forgiveness and patience.

"You know what else? I wasn't sure Jesus talked about past lives and that made me nervous at first. You remember that He is my special friend? So I like to run everything by Him. Sure enough, I did find some Bible stories that seemed to point to other lifetimes. As we kept talking about all this, especially how life is filled with lessons and choices, it started making more sense, like pieces of a puzzle fitting together. Like when you're mean, it shows you have more to learn. And when you're kind, it builds kindness that touches others.

"The wonderful thing is we all get as many chances as we need to be better people. The God force is very patient and loves you no matter what. It's inside of you, helping you choose to make this world a kinder, better place."

"But why?" asked Aurelia, still curious.

Edgar appreciated their listening. "Because all of us are here to learn, grow, and help each other. No matter what color your skin is, what language you speak, or how you pray. We are all equal and treasured by God. Our most important job is to be kind and loving. Because love heals. And best of all, love is exactly the same as God.

"And we also need to care for nature and the Earth. Because you know what? One day, we will all be back here again!"

"You mean in our next lifetime, right?" Lily asked.

"Indeed. When we are ready to learn more. How does that sound? Having many lives to learn from?" Edgar was curious what they made of all this.

The children were quiet. They loved to dress up. Now it would be even more fun, imagining other lifetimes.

James spoke up, "Well, if there is a next lifetime, I hope I'm the big brother. But right now, I'm hungry!"

"Heard that before!" said his big brother, Ryan, laughing.

"So am I," Edgar agreed. Indeed, it was supper time. "Let's all go to my garden and pick some vegetables for you to take home."

"Yay!" Cheering, James took off running. Aurelia helped Bodhi with his skipping. Lily and Eleanor stopped to pick flowers, and River and Ryan raced each other.

Juniper slipped her hand into Edgar's. "Thank you, Mr. Judge," she said quietly. "I think you must be the most wonderful man I know."

Edgar smiled fondly at her. "Ah, thank you, Junie. Helping others has been my purpose in life, all I've ever tried to do. It has been hard sometimes, but I know it's also a gift and one I am most happy to share.

"What I wonder is, what will you choose to do with your precious life? And how will you share love and kindness with other people? Those answers are inside of you. If you are patient, I know the answers will come to you. And they will be very, very good."

Then hand in hand, Edgar and Junie headed for the garden together in the late afternoon sun.

Karla Peterson and Leslie Cayce on a river rafting trip in Oregon

About the authors…

Karla Tedrick Peterson and Leslie Goodman Cayce met in Virginia Beach and have been close friends since 1975. Both have been helped throughout their lives by the wisdom found in the readings of Edgar Cayce.

Karla was first inspired by the Cayce work at the age of ten. She went on to earn a master's degree in public health, and raised her family at Lake Tahoe, California. Karla discovered a love of painting watercolors after her children left for college. Now the grandmother of four, she is excited to share stories with them about the spiritual lessons in Edgar Cayce's readings that have been so meaningful in her life.

Leslie married Charles Thomas Cayce, the grandson of Edgar Cayce, and has been actively involved in the Cayce work since college. Leslie holds a master's degree in social work, and is currently the President of the Edgar Cayce Foundation. She also serves on the A.R.E.'s Board of Trustees. She, too, has four grandchildren who want to hear more stories about their unusual and famous great-great-grandfather.

Karla and Leslie decided it was up to them to bring this book for children to life.

And so, this story was born.

NOTE: If you read this story to children, feel free to insert your young listeners' names for those in the story to increase their listening pleasure!

Manufactured by Amazon.ca
Bolton, ON